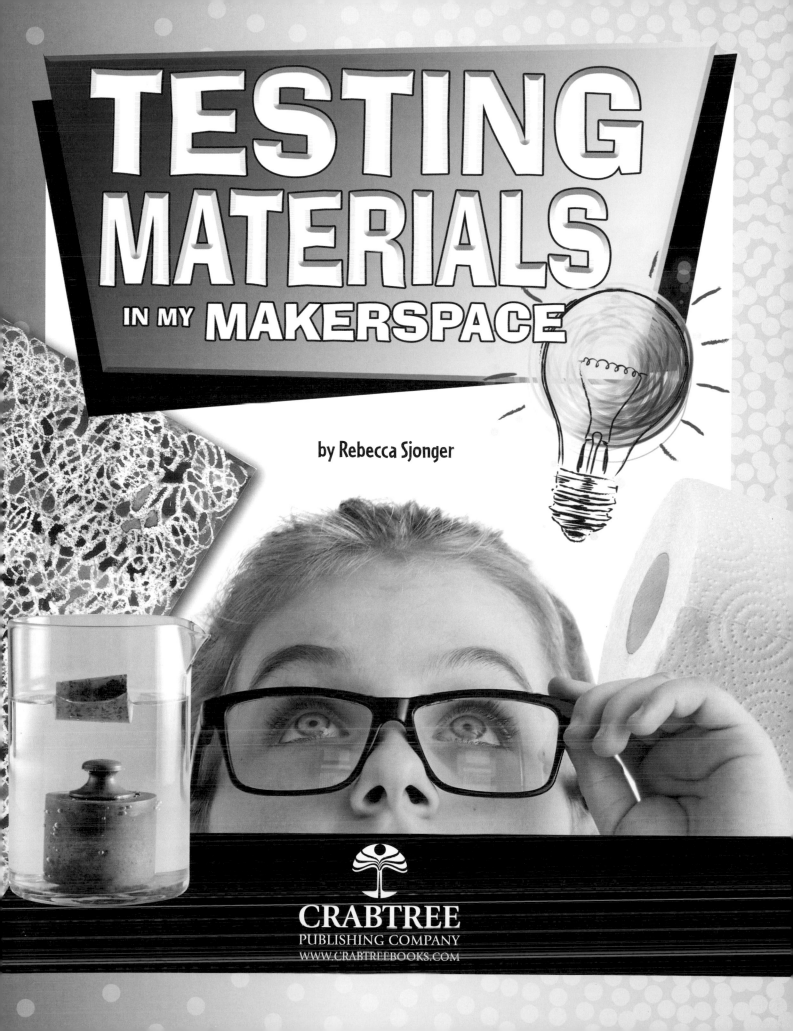

# TESTING MATERIALS
## IN MY MAKERSPACE

by Rebecca Sjonger

CRABTREE
PUBLISHING COMPANY
WWW.CRABTREEBOOKS.COM

# MATTER AND MATERIALS IN MY MAKERSPACE

**Author:**
Rebecca Sjonger

**Series research and development:**
Reagan Miller
Janine Deschenes

**Editorial director:**
Kathy Middleton

**Editor:**
Janine Deschenes

**Proofreader:**
Kelly Spence

**Design, photo research, and prepress:**
Katherine Berti

**Print and production coordinator:**
Katherine Berti

**Photographs:**
All images by Shutterstock

**Library and Archives Canada Cataloguing in Publication**

Sjonger, Rebecca, author
    Testing materials in my makerspace / Rebecca Sjonger.

(Matter and materials in my makerspace)
Includes index.
Issued in print and electronic formats.
ISBN 978-0-7787-4608-9 (hardcover).--
ISBN 978-0-7787-4624-9 (softcover).--
ISBN 978-1-4271-2048-9 (HTML)

    1. Materials--Testing--Juvenile literature.  2. Makerspaces--Juvenile
literature.  I. Title.

TA410.S56 2018        j620.1'10287        C2017-907634-5
                                          C2017-907635-3

**Library of Congress Cataloging-in-Publication Data**

Names: Sjonger, Rebecca, author.
Title: Testing materials in my makerspace / Rebecca Sjonger.
Description: New York, New York : Crabtree Publishing Company, [2018] |
    Series: Matter and materials in my makerspace | Includes index.
Identifiers: LCCN 2017057956 (print) | LCCN 2018005226 (ebook) |
    ISBN 9781427120489 (Electronic) |
    ISBN 9780778746089 (hardcover : alk. paper) |
    ISBN 9780778746249 (pbk. : alk. paper)
Subjects: LCSH: Materials--Properties--Juvenile literature. |
    Materials--Testing--Juvenile literature. |
    Materials--Experiments--Juvenile literature. | Makerspaces--Juvenile literature.
Classification: LCC QC173.36 (ebook) | LCC QC173.36 .S5656 2018 (print) |
    DDC  620.1/12--dc23
LC record available at https://lccn.loc.gov/2017057956

## Crabtree Publishing Company

www.crabtreebooks.com        1-800-387-7650

Printed in the U.S.A./032018/BG20180202

**Published in Canada**
**Crabtree Publishing**
616 Welland Ave.
St. Catharines, Ontario
L2M 5V6

**Published in the United States**
**Crabtree Publishing**
PMB 59051
350 Fifth Avenue, 59th Floor
New York, New York 10118

**Published in the United Kingdom**
**Crabtree Publishing**
Maritime House
Basin Road North, Hove
BN41 1WR

**Published in Australia**
**Crabtree Publishing**
3 Charles Street
Coburg North
VIC 3058

# CONTENTS

# YOU CAN BE A MAKER!

Who are makers? These people find creative ways to do tasks. They use everyday materials in new ways. Makers learn by testing these materials. The challenges in this book will help you choose materials to solve different problems and achieve different goals.

## TEAM UP

Makers often share their ideas, skills, and supplies. They work together in places called **makerspaces**. Your school or library may have one. If not, you could set up your own makerspace with some friends.

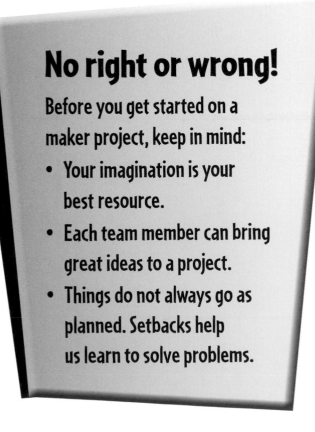

## No right or wrong!

Before you get started on a maker project, keep in mind:

- Your imagination is your best resource.
- Each team member can bring great ideas to a project.
- Things do not always go as planned. Setbacks help us learn to solve problems.

Working with other makers
means more ideas!

# MATTER AND MATERIALS

Every material you will test is made of **matter**. Matter is anything that takes up space and has **mass**. Mass is the amount of material in matter. We can find these materials in nature or make them ourselves.

## MATERIALS AND PROPERTIES

Maker projects use many different materials. They each have their own **properties**. These are the ways we describe materials, such as their size or shape. Studying the properties of materials helps makers sort and choose which ones to use.

## STATES OF MATTER

One property of a material is the **state**, or form, it takes. The two main states are **liquids** and **solids**. Liquids can be poured. They flow into the shape of whatever holds them. Solids keep their shape. They cannot be poured.

Milk is a liquid.
A glass is a solid.

## Try it!

Exploring the properties of materials will help you as a maker. Flip the page to learn more!

# EXPLORING PROPERTIES

A big part of testing materials is discovering their properties. There are many ways to do this. You could use a ruler to measure their size. Another helpful tool is a scale. It weighs materials to test how heavy they are. You could also use your senses! Look at each material. Touch it with your fingers. Could you taste, listen to, or smell it?

Ask an adult for permission before you taste or smell any materials, because some can be dangerous.

# PROPERTY CHALLENGE

Some materials are shown below. Explore and sort them based on these common properties.

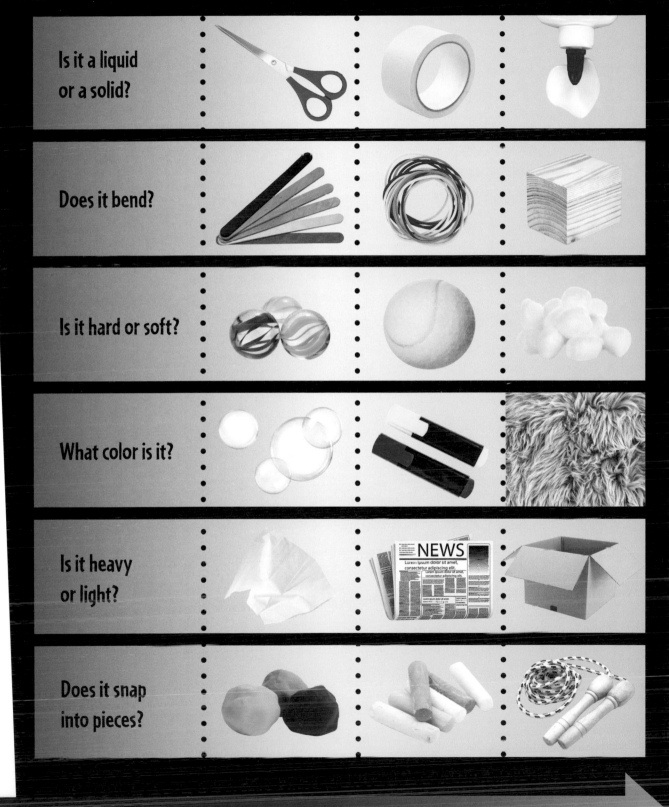

Is it a liquid or a solid?

Does it bend?

Is it hard or soft?

What color is it?

Is it heavy or light?

NEWS
Lorem ipsum dolor sit amet, consectetur adipiscing elit.

Does it snap into pieces?

Check out more properties on the next page!

# TESTING: ONE, TWO, THREE!

Makers examine the properties of materials to choose the best ones for each task. Imagine building a fort. Describe how each material would help to meet your goals. How could you test them?

## CLEAR AND OPAQUE

Would you want to see through the walls of your fort? How about the windows? You can see through some materials. They are **transparent**, or clear. Matter that you cannot see through is **opaque**. Other objects are in-between clear and opaque. You could use your sense of sight to test your building materials.

## HOW DOES IT FEEL?

Which materials could you use to make the inside of your fort comfortable? You could test them by feeling them. Soft **textures** feel good against your skin. Rough textures do not.

## Try it!

Build your own fort! Test your materials to make sure they suit, or fit, their purpose. Which other properties would you think about when making a fort? Flip back to Exploring Properties for ideas.

# MAKER TIPS

**Start every project by** brainstorming. **Take five minutes, and come up with as many ideas as you can think of. If you work with a team, listen to each person's ideas.**

## WHAT'S THE PLAN?

Choose one idea to start with. Kick off your project by making a plan. Draw your ideas and measure your materials. At each stage, be open to new ways of reaching your goal. Makers change plans if they can create something even better!

Listen to and respect the ideas of your team members.

12

| Material | Floats | Sinks |
|----------|--------|-------|
| rock | | ✓ |
| marble | | ✓ |
| plastic cup | ✓ | |

You could use a chart to keep track of your findings when you test materials for certain properties. Write the material on one side and the test results on another. Write down what happens.

## Help along the way

If you get stuck on a Maker Mission, here are some helpful hints:

- Do you understand the goal of the Maker Mission? Try saying it in your own words.

- Make sure every person on your team understands the plan.

- Use what you learn in each mission to make other projects better!

# DOES IT ABSORB?

Some solids absorb, or soak up, liquids. For example, a sponge soaks up a lot of water. Have you ever spilled a drink on a book? If so, you know that some papers can absorb liquids, too!

## PAPER THAT ABSORBS

Which kind of paper would you use to wipe up a spill? Paper towel works well for this task. This material soaks up a lot of liquid. It is also a good size and strength for the job. Test it yourself!

## PAPER THAT REPELS

Other solids do not soak up liquids. Some papers **repel**, or keep away, liquids. Glossy or waxy materials repel water. Adding glossy or waxy materials to paper helps it repel liquids, too. That is why you would not wipe up water with a postcard! Study the covers of books and magazines. Why do you think they use special paper?

Crayons made the waxy layer that repelled the paint in this picture.

## Try it!

Test materials that absorb and repel by making a poster. Get started on the next page! Brainstorming designs will help you with this Maker Mission.

# MAKE IT REPEL

**MAKER MISSION**

Create a cool poster! Test materials and find a way to make words or pictures show up when you paint on top of them. You will need to use a material that repels paint to create your design.

## Materials

- Paper
- Pencil
- White art paper
- Art supplies, such as light-colored crayons, oil pastels, colored pencils
- Watercolor paints
- Paintbrushes
- Container of water

# THINK ABOUT IT

## Materials

Is it important to test your materials before making the poster? Why or why not?

Which materials might create a waxy layer that could repel liquid?

## Design

Which colors will show up well when used together?

## Size

Should you start with a lot of water on your paintbrush, or just a little?

### MISSION ACCOMPLISHED

Did your materials repel the paint? If not, what other materials could you try? Would it help to use a more or less waxy material?

When your poster is picture perfect, check out Endless Ideas on page 30.

# HOT OR COLD?

Matter can change states! Heat an egg in a frying pan and what happens? The liquid egg becomes a solid! One of the properties of matter is the temperature at which it changes states.

## CHANGING STATES

Some liquids become solid when they cool down. For example, you can make ice cream by freezing milk. Some solids become a liquid when they warm up. This explains why ice cream melts as it becomes warm.

Delicious slushies are made mostly of frozen water.

Handles protect fingers from hot mugs.

## HANDLING HEAT

Materials have another property related to temperature. Some pass heat to other materials. Picture a mug of warm hot chocolate. Does the mug get warm, too? When this happens, it passes the heat from the liquid outward. This causes the hot chocolate to cool down. Some mugs use padding materials to keep in heat. These materials stop or slow down heat as it moves from one material to another.

This knitted sleeve keeps the liquid inside the cup from losing heat.

## Try it!

Head to the challenge on the next page to explore these properties and test materials. Remember to plan before you get to work.

# MAKE IT CuOL—AND WArM!

Make a warm drink container that keeps in the heat. You need to be able to hold it in your hand safely and comfortably. The drink must stay warm for at least five minutes.

## Materials

- Paper
- Pencil
- Scissors
- Clean container made from glass, plastic, or Styrofoam
- Padding materials, such as felt, bubble wrap, or cardboard
- Joining material, such as tape
- Warm drink, such as hot chocolate

## MAKE IT SAFE

Ask an adult to help you make a warm drink. Be sure not to touch any hot materials with your bare hands!

# THINK ABOUT IT

### Materials

How could warm water help you test your materials?

### Design

Who could you ask to help you prepare the warm drink and test your design?

What kind of solid container do you think might pass on the most heat? Test a few!

What padding materials will you use to keep in the heat?

How will you attach the padding materials to the container?

### Size

Do you need enough warm liquid for one test or multiple tests?

## MISSION ACCOMPLISHED

Was your container cool enough to hold? Did it keep your drink warm for at least five minutes?

When your creation works well, check out Endless Ideas on page 30.

# HoW sTRoNG Is IT?

Makers test how strong materials are before using them. Strength is a property of solids. Stronger ones take longer to break down. Why do you think this is helpful for maker projects?

## PROPERTY POWER

Other properties affect how strong materials are. For example, a hard material is usually stronger than a soft material. What other properties could you explore? To start your list, think about size and shape. You can also join materials with different properties to add strength.

## STRUCTURE STRENGTH

Strength is important when you make a **structure**. A bridge, a table, and a swing set are all structures. They are put together using strong materials, such as wood or metal. You may be surprised by how storng some materials are! For example, hard-packed snow makes a sturdy snow fort.

This snow fort is made strong by stacking blocks of snow that are about the same size.

## Try it!

Are you ready to test materials and make your own strong structure? Get started on the next page! Stick with your project even if it doesn't work out on the first try.

# MAKE A STRONG STRUCTURE

Make a structure that is strong enough to support your body weight. It must be at least 1 foot (30 cm) tall. The structure must not break apart when you stand on it.

## Materials

- Paper
- Pencil
- Ruler
- Wooden materials, such as blocks of wood
- Metal materials, such as pails
- Plastic materials, such as tubs
- Joining materials, such as glue

### MAKE IT SAFE

If you want to use any tools, make sure you ask an adult for help. Make sure an adult is there when you test your structure by standing on it, too.

# THINK ABOUT IT

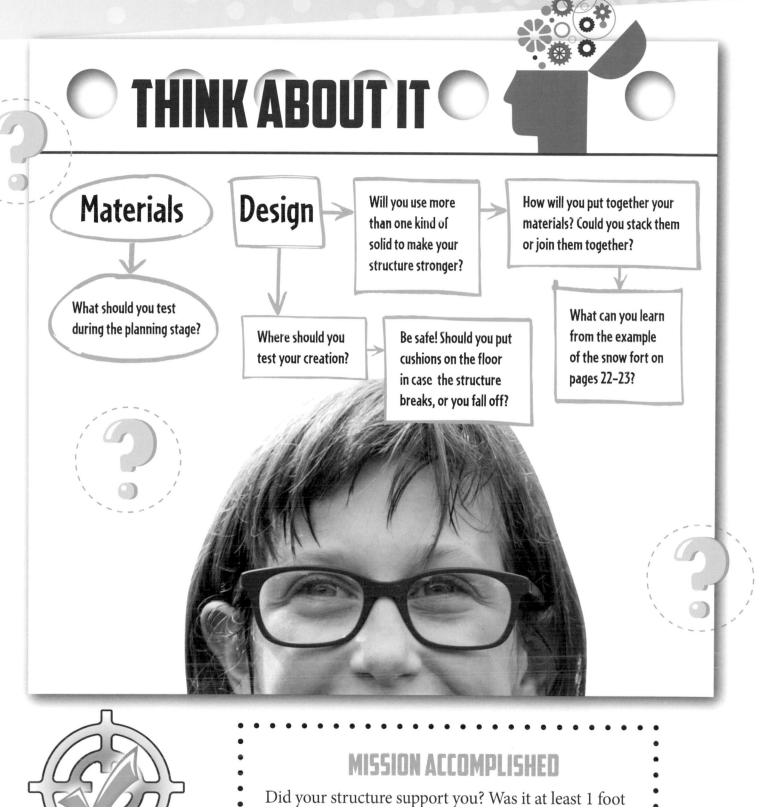

**Materials**

What should you test during the planning stage?

**Design**

Will you use more than one kind of solid to make your structure stronger?

How will you put together your materials? Could you stack them or join them together?

Where should you test your creation?

Be safe! Should you put cushions on the floor in case the structure breaks, or you fall off?

What can you learn from the example of the snow fort on pages 22–23?

## MISSION ACCOMPLISHED

Did your structure support you? Was it at least 1 foot (30 cm) tall? If not, test your materials and design to look for more ideas. Then build on what you made.

Flip to page 30 for some ideas.

# WHAT HAPPENS IN WATER?

Do you like to test what floats and what sinks? These are also properties of materials! Remember, matter has mass. Solids float if they have less mass than the liquids they are in. They sink if they have more mass than the liquids.

## KEEP OUT THE WATER

Solids that do not absorb water float better. Test this the next time you are in the tub. Dunk a cloth and a plastic toy in the water. Which one do you think will float?

Some materials made from plastic, such as this duck, float in water.

## SIZE AND SHAPE MATTER

Try an experiment with play dough. Flatten it and place it in water. Then, roll it into a ball. Put it back in the water to see if it acts the same. The properties of shape and size affect sinking and floating!

## Try it!

Test floating and sinking in the challenge on the next page. Start by brainstorming creative ways to use solids.

The materials that make up this boat were specially chosen to help it float!

# MAKE IT FLOAT

Make a boat that floats in water! Your creation must not sink when you place an apple on it.

## Materials

- Paper
- Pencil
- Building supplies, such as corks, juice carton, foil or Styrofoam trays
- Tape, elastics, metal clips
- Scissors
- Large tub of water for testing
- Apple

# THINK ABOUT IT

## Design

Why would drawing your ideas be helpful?

## Size

What should you measure?

Do the size and shape of your boat matter?

## Materials

What should you test before you choose your materials?

Does it matter whether the materials you use to join the parts of your boat absorb water?

## MISSION ACCOMPLISHED

Did your boat stay afloat with an apple on it? Flip back to the Maker Tips on page 12 if you need help.

When you are done, there are more floating challenges on the next page.

# ENDLESS IDEAS

What will you make next?
Get started with these ideas:

pages 20–21

## Make it repel

pages 16–17

- What materials could you use other than a waxy one? Which kinds of glue might work on the bottom layer?
- Test different kinds of papers to see which absorb and repel the same art materials.

## Make it cool— and warm!

- Switch it around! Could you keep a material such as ice cream from melting?
- Which changes would you need to make to your first design?

## Make a strong structure

pages 24–25

- Try building a structure that holds two or more people. Work with a team!
- How could you use the same materials to make a structure for a different purpose?

## Make it float

pages 28–29

- Think bigger! How could you make a boat that supports twice the load?
- What else would be fun to float? How about a floating comic book holder for the bathtub?

# LEARNING MORE

## BOOKS

Guillain, Charlotte. *Comparing Properties*. Heinemann Library, 2009.

Mason, Adrienne. *Touch It! Materials, Matter and You*. Kids Can Press, 2005.

Rustad, Martha. *What Is It Made Of? Noticing Types of Materials*. Millbrook Press, 2015.

## WEBSITES

Check out more ways to test how solid and liquid art materials absorb and repel at:
**https://artfulparent.com/2015/05/6-watercolor-resist-techniques-to-try.html**

Get ideas for other strong structures you could make at:
**http://pbskids.org/designsquad/build**

Find out about how to hold in heat with the activities at:
**www.scholastic.com/magicschoolbus/parentteacher/activities/arctic.htm**

Do you think eggs float? Try this experiment and find out:
**www.sciencefun.org/kidszone/experiments/floating-egg**

# GLOSSARY

**absorb** To soak up a liquid

**brainstorm** To list many ideas—no matter how silly—as quickly as possible

**liquid** Matter that can be poured and takes on the shape of its container

**makerspace** A place where makers work together and share their supplies and skills

**mass** The measurable amount of material in matter

**material** Any substance that makes up matter

**matter** Any material that takes up space and has mass

**opaque** Describes matter that is not see-through

**property** A characteristic that describes matter

**repel** To keep away a material

**solid** Matter that does not flow and cannot be poured

**state** The form that matter takes, such as a solid or a liquid

**structure** An object that is built using solid materials

**temperature** The measure of how hot or cold something is

**texture** The look or feel of an object, such as soft or rough

**transparent** Describes matter that is clear and see-through

# INDEX

## ABOUT THE AUTHOR

Rebecca Sjonger is the author of more than 50 children's books. She has written numerous titles for the *Be a Maker!* and the *Simple Machines in My Makerspace* series.